SOUL

ESTATES

Poetry by

JIRI JIRASEK

IN Publications

2010

IN PUBLICATIONS
14 Lorraine Circle
Waban, MA 02468

Second edition 2010

Cover Art: Kaline Charrey

SOUL ESTATES, ISBN: 978-0-9819797-4-8

SECTIONS

Languid transparency of love's potential
Rippling on the curved surface of desire
Invites waiting
While existence is pregnant
                            with Nothingness…

FAWN INTERLUDES

FAWNS

When the sun undresses
Taking off the pelerine of clouds
And steps into the evening bath
Of night
We might be lucky
To be kissed by its passing light
While undressing
The moon in flight
Through our dreams -
Like pelerines
Rippling on the mountain crests
While morning rests
In un-cried dew
Of silent flowers.
With our palms
We caress precious hours
Of our few - but happy dawns -
And if we are really lucky,
Cuddly fawns may glimpse
Around the corner of our day.
That should be enough:
Fawns will never stay.
But we are getting tough,
Aren't we?

INVITATION

You do not have to
Lose yourself
While loving me -
Since I will always be
Your country
Of my open heart -
Guarding flowers
Of my meadows
For you to pick and weave
And share my forests
For our storms
Which would dare
Our very mountains.

You do not have to
Lose yourself
While loving me -
You can rather
Find yourself anew
In our fountains
Of our clarity of mind.
I will find myself in you -
So - leave your fears behind -
And love, and trust -
And be - together!

NAME

You signed your name
Into the snow
But I expect
Flowers to grow
Soon into your letters
To be read as an invitation
To spring
And offering of your love.

EARLY SPRING

I caught your quick glance back
When I turned my head
To see you slip away
Through trains and plains
And schedules of the Earth.

There was not a shortcut space
In between -
In place of translucency
Of our glow -
We know how to grow on.

So when you return to my arms
I will open all my farms
To horses of my joy
To roam through and round
And in your heart
Of sacred temples of your trust!
It is the least for an early spring
And it is a must
As my offering of love.
(Besides, it is pure fun.)

LAYER CAKE

Layers of green breaths
Upon layers of sunshine
Upon layers of consciousness!
The loving inter-stratification
Of karma upon human needs -
Mon Bijou of your female body
Upon layers of my spiritual lust
Accumulated through my
Centuries of waiting for you;
That is our layer cake
For our zero birthday
Of the beginning of our love!

SUBLIMINAL SYMPHONIES

You may still not hear
The subliminal symphony of my soul
But I am playing it for you
At the shore of conscious love
Where our thoughts can barely tread
Wearing shoes of daily reason -
But it is our music season
And the music is our own.

Do you play a symphony for me?
(since you may play one, as well.)
I just want to hear the spell
Of our careful conductor
(unless you are without one!)
Our symphonies will always run
                    their course
Whispering down through the 'dolce'
                    parts
Before coming like a storm
In the finale of endless movements.
Attunements to subtle harmonies
Will make us start to listen
To our subliminal symphonies -
Since neither of us really cares
For the hard rock of the day.
So play for me, my darling, play!

4

MORNING

You look combed by the sun
And smoothed by the lake
When I wake up with you
And take each day new
As a gift for both of us
To unwrap and wear
Throughout the day -
And through our nights together,
To bathe in love
And swim in lagoons of dreams
Of our new mornings
Full of the sun -
Renewed
In crystalline light
Of our being.

SYLLABLES

Waking up
To your hug and kiss
Is like bliss of spring
When hibernation is over
And rivulets
Of bird song cheers
Are syllables
Of whispered love.
Only half of this
Would make me happy:
Finding finally four-leaf clover -
So when the rest
Of spring appears -
I am sold on love
Above my own subliminal
Doubts...

PLAYING

Our symphonies
Are arabesques of feelings
Carved out of our dreams
Of subconscious longing
For our consciousness
Of peace -
Where bliss
Can bubble out and over
In any octave of pure joy
Of playing without conductor
In harmony with being.
Hearing subtle harmonies of silence
Will prick our listening souls
And playing along
In our hearts
Will set our goals for a future...
...since neither of us really cares
For the hard rock of the day; -
So play for me, my darling, play!

START OF FUTURE

You are the rainbow
To my rain -
You are the soothing
To my pain -
You are the colours
To my painting -
You are the catalyst
Calibrating
To my living rich
Through the music
Of our life.
You can teach me:
You are the poet,
I am your fan -
With heart bursting
Till the end...
Yet, you are the start
Of boldness
Of our future world
To live.

POEM TO MY MISTRESS

I will take the cords
Of your touches
From your fingers and your lips
If you keep on offering
Your lips and fingers
And reapply them
To the beat
Of my body's heat;
My body's heat may attune
To beginnings of springs
With the underlying melody
Of your undulation -
So keep on undulating
Melody of senses -
While the ocean of your eyes
Will ripple with
The higher octaves
Of our passion shared -
Since you also shared your hurting
And your sighs -
Unheard by many -
Will reverberate
Through my registers of feelings,
So my feelings may start
Welcoming you back -
While the healing
Of our hearts
Will let our souls
Go free of pain
While your heart will recover just now
From the thorns of my roses…
Our domain of love
Is here to stay -
Let us cherish it somehow
Before destiny takes its course;
Yet our source is true -
Always!

LAKE

Lakes are peaceful
Like innocent eyes of fawns
When the dew is rising to the sun
In countless days
Of miniature rainbows.
And when the sun will outline
Fluffy horizons with distant trees
You will have nothing but the reveries
Of soaring flight
Because the very lake
You have within your sight
Is the lake with ever rising sun -
And you will be one with its calm
Inviting you beyond time.
You will be one with light
Where no harm
Can ever reach you.

YONDER

To learn the language
Of your silence! -
Or to at least read it right -
To see your inner truth
With my inner sight
And answer it through wisdom
While producing our joy.
To let it flow
And let it bounce -
To let it bounce between
Our hearts -
To let it go
Beyond our doubts
And shoot down darts
Of intellect and fear…
Come to me
And speak your silence
Softer than you do,
Come to me so near
That islands of my weakness
Will disappear
Like kites in the yonder
Of sky.

6

LOOKING

I was looking for you
In many women's smiles
But I missed your voice.
I was looking for you
In many women's faces
But I missed your eyes.
I was looking for you
In many women's hearts
But I missed your soul!
They had loved me their own way
But I could not love them mine:
You are the only one to stay
To see my love soon start to shine.

PRAYING

I am praying
(if that is at all possible)
I am praying
To your female soul
(if that is also possible)
To pour over me your love
Like when your naked body
Glides over mine at night -
And remove all my pain
(which is quite impossible)
(as if slaying dragons
from without
would turn poor frog
into a prince)
But I am praying
To your soul
To let me in
And rest awhile
Before facing
God.

DELAYED SPRING

Weeping ledges
Of stony buildings
Soaking wet with
Rivulets of rain -
Twisting strands
Of tangled hairdos
Of fleeting women
Beyond pain...
Melted windows
Full of faces
Blind to their own shapes -
Shapeless mirrors -
Ghostly shadows
Waiting for their fate...
Fallen leaves in puddles
Stuck to footsteps
Without people -
Drown in dark
In autumn day -
Glowing dimly
Through the crystal -
Broken bottles
Made of clay -
And women gone
Behind the corners...

Yet some of them
Have sweetest fragrance
Lingering with sun
In their hair
Of warmth
And comfort.

OTHER SIDE

You can take my music
Safely to your bed:
It will caress you to sleep
And your dreams beyond...
And if it met your hopes
And you can meet my own
I would like to find you
On the other side of dreams.

MATING

I will offer you my fingers
Through the wings of music
And you can use them
Any time your magic dissipates.

I will comb your hair
Through my tunes and melodies
And you can get all this
If you are mine -
And the fates will bring us back.

I will caress you with love
Through my soul and flame
And you can be the same
All the time - since we are mates -
And we will mate again
And yet again.

GATES TO LIFE

In the abstract mansions
Of my shifted-ego-self
I create new sounds
For your poetry!
They are growing
On a crystal tree of love
And I just pick and blend
Their bells and purple violins
At violet skylights of my feelings.
If you are healing
Let me know -
So I may abolish all snow
In our cosmic paradise.
Let the heart-shine rise
Way over the mountains
Of our human sorrows!
It is all right to borrow
From our visions of pure faith
If the gates to life
Open in this world.

DOVE

You can hear air humming
You can feel birds coming
You can touch the light
A miracle of flight!
Can you match your love?
A golden-white soft dove!

PLANETARY VISION

One day we will find
Our hugging place
In the kissing valley
Of our smooching planet
And will celebrate the sun
Through our singing skins
In our titillating meadow
On our teasing hill
Through our liberated fingers
In the softest grass
With the guards of flowers
Through our gourmet kisses
In the summer breeze
In the air of forest
Through our fruity nibbles
With the tooting birds
With the butterfly's own pageant
Through our lustful scooping
With the birch trees snooping
With the skinny-dipping clouds
Through our passion's merging
With the nature verging
On a climax of the woods
In our love-enchanted country
Of our karmic roots
On our soul-fulfilling planet
In the universe that flipped!

AQUAMARINE SPACE

There is aquamarine space
Where liquid sunrays
Melt the music within mind -
So dimensions will open wide -
Just beyond mind's bend
Where space will levitate to light
And feelings turn to birds of colours
All in flight
Nibbling gently at the soft white sand
Of your private beach
To aquamarine waves of warmth
Just beneath your feet
Without bending anything - but light
To produce hues of love.

UNIVERSAL LOVE

I love you
Like the clouds love
Clear blue sky
But with an emphasis
Of lightning.

I love you
Like the hills love
Countryside
But with a dimension
Of mountains.

I love you
Like the rain loves
Soaking earth
But with a potency
Of oceans -

And I love you
Like the Earth loves the universe
With emotions and motions
But humble in my trust.

YOU ARE LOVED

I feel you
Through the texture
Of my dreams
When I cannot feel you
With my hands.

I hug you
Through the humming trees
When I cannot hug you
With my arms.

I rock you
Through the skipping brooks
When I cannot rock you
With my body.

And I live with you
Beyond my present means
In my boldest future
Of my sharing.

Am I daring
Loving you far outside of time?
But that way
You are loved already now!

REASONS

In the contrast
To my days
Full of
Interstellar void
You now feel like
Solid gold to me -
Yet I see
A festive difference
From the other seasons…
Do you need my reasons
For loving you?

TIP OF FULFILLMENT

At one pointed point
Of fleetingly obscured 'now'
You were my woman
In love -
In love with me,
Since I was your man
For that transient ever-time
Of immature spring
And non-existent summer
With some of the cosmically
           pubic hope
Spilling into
A possible ongoing purpose
Of our life jail sentence
As humans…

You were a beautiful silver
Cry with a golden lining
Shining in your midnight eyes
When silence of your lips
Turned my need for existence
Into a tip of fulfillment
And a touch, a sense, of happiness
Amidst your
Flights with me
To oblivion.

IS IT IN OUR HEADS?

I do not even need your body
For loving you -
But it would help
To feel your soul -
If not your love.

But maybe it is all
In our heads
And we need
Our tired bodies
For lovemaking -
And only our minds
Long to escape
To resonant essences
           of beauty
Of lakes beyond water
Trees beyond leaves
And fingers of love
Beyond touch
           of fingers.

PIGEONS

At those times
When the dawn is unfolding
Its foggy scarves of rain
And greying pigeons
Come to sit behind the
                    window panes
Of my bedroom -
The building itself
Somehow opens
Its illusory concrete heart
                    for them
And then they start
To say my name -
In their pigeon language,
As if calling me in vain -
While you are lying there,
At those times,
Right next to me and silent -
Never different,
But never quite the same...

HOW COME?

If you are only a human being,
How come I am seeing
The waiting universe
In the silence before
Your unasked question?

If you are only a working woman,
How come all the true men
Sense the paradise
In your body
Before your withheld embrace?

And
If you are only a humble friend,
How come you feel sent
To me by angels -
To love now
Before my unsaid promise?

You are a child
Who needs to grow a garden
Within your own heart -
And
I am a gardener
Who is looking
For a garden
To tend to
For his soul.

If you are only a part of life,
How come I feel whole with you?

WAITING

Waiting for you
Is like moonlight spilled
On the silver waves
Of the midnight lake
With no moon in the sky.

Waiting for you
Is like rainbow pierced
Through the rainy clouds
With no sun
Shining bright and high.

Waiting for you
Is like the timeless quest
Of any restless mind
With the crest of time
Nibbling at my cry...

Why do we ask for eternity?

MESSAGE

I will seal
Some happiness
In a pebble
Of my hope
And throw it
In the universe
Like a message
In a bottle
For your God
To read.

MESSAGE IN A BOTTLE

When you find this message
Sent out in a bottle
Do not send me a ship!
Just try to find my island
By heart...
(by *your* heart)
And come to stay in sun
If you dare -
Alone as I am -
Naked as I am -
Barefoot, bare-souled,
Whole - yet incomplete!

LET'S FLOAT

You - the sea of energy
Splashing at my shore
Of continuous hope…!
Let's float
With surfs of need,
Let's make it
A unanimous vote!

FLOATING

You are in my mind
Like the summer -
But also summer storms
Charging up my nights.

You are in my heart
Like a river
But also river whirlpools
Pulling me to depths unknown.

Through your eyes
I have flown
To the edge of death
But life in Light
Was beyond there
And clearly waiting.
Do I dare
Have you in my soul?
Please just care for me
And stroll in my fearful
Happy dreams -
Goals are best untold
When one's spontaneous bliss
Can book free tickets
To shared paradise
(return ticket
for the price
we are now paying).

In the summer of your love
I will check the rates
Of hearts,
Unfrequented beaches
Of the longest reaches
Of your playful seas to float…

FLOW

Where does the flow go -
How fast does it flow?
How slow does my love grow -
Do I ever know?
Do I aid the flow,
Letting my heart overflow
         with love?
Or do I starve my soul
Having my identity
Under-flowed by half?!
By the better half
Of the universe,
By *you* - my female
Principle -
Where principles
      do not count
And law is only one;
One with the flow!
Let me softly chant
Let my love still grow.

I'LL FLOW WITH YOU IN STILLNESS

If I could
Re-create the diamonds
Of the rising sun
In my setting tears
I would make
My midnight fears
Subject to your love.
You - being
The queen of longing
And I - being
The king of nothingness -
My tears are flowing
To your sea of bliss
Where all the waters
Of this world
Are sacred -
Because of their flow.
How far can I go -
Once my tears dry up
With no more diamonds left
To transfer into streams?
It all seems like flow of living time
Will continue
To mark its confluence
With light.
If you throw your diamonds
In my brand new star
I would erase
Scars of grief
By taking you past reefs of ever
So you would never
Be a queen
Of human longing…

ABORTED MOON

If I wake up
From the aborted moon
Splitting my hemispheres
Into a sweet singing void
Of forgotten wisdom -
You have me here:
Utterly trusting child
Of your willingness
To suspend economy
Of reason
For the benefit of seasons
Of innocence of a minute
                    or two -
Of your own forgotten
                    childhood.
Your star may have you flown
Through my universe at night
Where you may have recognized
Your own aborted moon -
Yet soon you will grow the moon
                    with me
And then we will sleep
Its fullness happily,
                    ever after.

TIME

Thank you for your time
Which is more than
Time sharing
Between the two of us-
Time in - time out,
Time inside-out
And unspoken
Incorporated
Timeless time
Of instants
Through instances
Beyond time -
Now and again.

So, from time to time
Let us time
Our moments together
To have good times -
Or at least
Time of our lives,
Forever now,
Or for the present time -
And without
A time limit.

DOOR

I miss you in my world
And I miss you in yours -
Because I miss myself there;
And because I miss you
To an extent I love you -
I must be loving you more
Than when I used to miss you
Once a week...
The trick to time
Is to live in now
But how will I get you
In my time
Without taking yours away?
I miss you every day,
Yet want you not to miss me badly,
Only enough - to be gladly mine -
And often -
And be perhaps happier
Than many times before...
I still miss the door
To your world -
But as you heard mine already
Open to you rather wide -
Shall we hide in security
Of our worlds
Or shall we reconstruct them
Into one for both?

HOME

My home is a state of mind -
Therefore, it is portable and free -
But my state of mind depends on life
And my private world
Which surrounds me so far.
I used to be alone with my need to share
And therefore I could become homeless
                                    now and then.
It was when
My aloneness and loneliness would
                                    merge
Into the hunger of soul of every man.
With you in my life
I am not alone any more
And therefore - being homeless
Is in the distant past -
So even hunger of the soul
Will get a quite new meaning -
And feeding it together
We will make our home at last.

MANTRA

Books are but mere words
When the meaning escapes us -
A meaning of life
Is but mere survival
When mantras of love
Do not germinate
The right way...
But my mind brought me
The mantra of your name
And it germinated
In my soul
Beyond my efforts
To water it.

LIGHTLY

I think of you lightly
Like a passing summer breeze
Touches the lazy tops of trees
And a butterfly may kiss
A rock next to the meadows;
Like a brook would lick the ferns
Yet unbound by their shadows.

LATE SUMMER

Late summer
Came too soon
With a translucent
Dress of your mood
Of unfulfilled
Spring lingering
In your mind…
… I will never
Find a pair
Of shoes to match
The dress
Of your blues.

GONE

While I am gone
I will be with you
All the same
Because your hair
Would remember
My hand
As my ears
Will remember
Your laughter
When we embraced
With an ease
Of Siamese twins.

SOFT RAIN

Soft rain descended
On my empty palm
Turning it into
A lush green park
Which was my dream
Of the world
For today.

I was still alone -
Only some white birds
Were playing golf
Among the trees.

Your palm did not reach
My rain
And your eyelashes
Did not catch a bird
In flight.
You stayed dry -
Hidden in my dream,
In a breezy desert sun.

TO GOD
& MY PLAYFUL LOVER

Un-thought
And unspoken -
Games within games:
I read them all,
Playing along -
Loving you, love -
Throughout and true,
Loving you till the end
Which never comes…

BLOOMING

Discovering zest for life
Feels so right with you -
As right as our gorgeous spring
Bringing offering of budding flowers
Which cannot wait to cuddle with the
                    sun
(as we cannot wait to cuddle
                    with each other).
Your soul seems to be as warm -
And if I was your brother -
You will not open all your petals
As your petals bloom
Into a rose for my stem
And I will slowly learn
To love you
As my woman
Of the soul.
So, I may notice all the clues of fears
You may even deny to your mind
As long as you can respond in kind
And talk to me beyond your touch.

I WILL

I will see it through your eyes -
As your eyes would see beyond
                    the scope
Of the slope of mountains
                    passing by…

I will feel it through your skin -
As your skin would sense the breeze
                    of space
Interlacing dimensions both deep
                    and high…

I will happen through your heart -
As your heart would find the truth
                    of life
Striving for the realness till we die.

I will be and I will not cry
Accepting the gifts of love!

MAGIC

Golden leaves are falling down
While you look up to the tree-tops
Resting your hand on my arm
And I am with you again…

Fog has lifted from the sun
So its rays are painting magic
Through the woods of autumn charm
And I am with you again…

Gentle breeze is soft and warm
When you kiss me at the cliff-side
Feeling safe from any harm
And I am with you again…

Then a swarm of 'birds-&-bees'
Would descend on your palm
From the translucence of calm
And you want to run and laugh
And run, and run, and run -
To fragrant meadows -
Where my arms do catch you
In a balmy embrace -
One so loving and so warm
That you let your silver laughter
Burst in joyous fountain spring
                    of fun -
And I am with you again…
Accepting the magic
You have done
For both of us: new lovers.

AUTUMN FLIGHT

You took my feelings
For a flight
Through your night and day...
And back again.
I hope your pain will not stay
                              in vain
So speak to me
Of distant stars
And I may resonate
                    for you
Far, yet closer
To your being
In a distant light.
Our time is also getting closer...
Shall I be your kite?

ONLY THE CLOUDS

Who knows all
Your day-dreams?
Only the clouds
Drifting through
Your eyes...

SEAWAVES

I wished
And you gave me your sea-waves,
I wished
And you showed me your strands,
I wished
And you shared
Your night skies,
I wish
That it never ends...

In the sea-waves time just sleeps
Its ways of eternity noisy,
In tree-sways
Winds underscore the birds,
In the cloud-drifts
Skies go soaking blue
To soothe their voids tranquilly,
In the mind shifts
Happiness tries to outweigh hurts.

I wish to give you time
Of the sea-waves -
I wish to give you songs
Of the trees -
I wish to give you calm
Of the azure -
I wish my happiness
Would show and please.

SEA-SURFS

In the sea-surfs
Titillating seconds
Breed like ripples -
In the tree-tops
Breezes circulate
Their silver strands -
In the cloud-shifts
Horizons touch
Hill-top nipples -
In the mind lakes
We go swimming
With our hands.

AUTUMN PERSPECTIVE

The colours of fall - sculptured
By golden-red leaves
Give transient warmth
To the dying greens -
Yet memories are set
In the dream-framed
Meadow forests
Of eternal summer and heat
Where explicit
Details are not needed
To appreciate the equinox
Of spring,
Springing from love.

FUTURE SYMPHONIES

Piano for waterfall
And silence -
When the song and dance
Are fading echoes
Of our mating -
But music
Is still waiting...
Since music never stops
In future symphonies
Of the confluence
And flow of innocence
Through our memories
Of peace
When love is but a lease
On life.

WHEN YOU RETURN

When you return to me
With your eyes
Full of enormous skies
Of crimson sunsets
And your hair
Full of powerful mists
Of majestic mountains
And your palms
Lonely of good-byes
Far gone, yet full of
Tenderness for me...
You will be returning to your man
And you will be ready to listen
To your own need
In your open heart -
Because I will tell you
That I love you
Because I know you will
Do the same -
Knowing how -
When you return to me
To be my woman.

BUBBLES

Welcome to my sunny bubble.
I snatched it greedily
Like a hungry creature would
Go after food.
I was in a mood for life;
It is a precious benign time
With sunshine sweeping
The local universe of Nature
Cleaning darker corners
Of one's mind
In the interim.

It is a whim of existence
No more than a catastrophe
Due for centuries
By a chance of human
Tempered estimates.
A sunny bubble
Before some more rain and clouds -
A blue taste of hope
Before your renewed doubts…
A subliminal song of wind
Before a ruthless storm
A hint of utopia's norm
Before the daily world
You abhor
Comes back with the news:
Blues of principles of peace
Before the 'yet another war'
Out there…

You never understand
From your inward stand
While lashing with your senses
Tuned to living green.
Why are we to dream
In bursting bubbles
While the background
Looms as black
As Nothingness?
Is it because this
Is what the Nature
Of the very universe
Of ours truly is?

Is the whole of existence
But a mere light dance
Of bubbles
Of the passing thoughts
In the consciousness
Of God?

But then again:
Our subtlest visions
Can sometimes perhaps
Out-dream
Even Him…

THERE COMES THE TIME

There is a time in our lives
When there is no dew left
To water the desert of our souls
With tears of happiness
- or so it seems...

There is a time in our dreams
When there are no birds left
To fly through our thoughts
And tired calm sits in our wounds
- or so it feels.

But there comes the time in our minds
When space of nothingness itself
Opens up to let the need of feeling
Fill our thirsty hearts
Inviting love
- and so it is.

DREAMING

Sometimes, when you abandon
Yourself
In a hot stream
Of exploding stars -
I may become
Your universe
For a while -
Sometimes -
By virtue of God's purpose
In your human flesh
I dance with you
Only to wake up
From my dreaming
Of our future lives
When we will really love
Each other freely.

END OF SEASON

Distant barking
Of a dog
Got stuck behind
A piece of bark
While a yellow leaf
Of fall
Zigzagged slowly
On my lap.
A lamp-post
Of a dandelion
Snapped its stem in half
As a sudden gust of wind
Blew its whitish fluff -
Switching off its light.
The sun was kissing me
Good-night
At the end of summer season.
I could get no single reason
To refuse.
How do you argue
With the clouds?

TIMELESSNESS

I want you to be
A cool refreshing
Waterfall
To my parched
Desert rocks
Of time
(within this timelessness)
If you only
Hold my hand
A little bit longer
Than forever now
Which threatens
To be (lost?)...

QUESTION

Is life but a butterfly
Touching here and touching there,
Nowhere to go -
But nowhere to stay?
Or are there flowers in our lives,
After the sunset -
And beyond the midnight,
Where butterflies would live
Next day?

OBSERVATION

I felt the depth of your need
In your intermittent silence
And future happiness of wisdom
In your relaxed tear.
Our fear will not keep us
Separate islands
If we acknowledge
The sea is clear...

TWO HAIKU

Born to touch the world
You are growing flower;
Knowledge in your heart.

May your time be sweet -
Tasting like the wine
Sipped from cup of music.

COLLATERAL

LOVE

YOU MAY THINK

You may think
You poured the wine -
Yet the cup is empty…

AN AFTERTHOUGHT

I never told you
How I loved you
Because I loved you
Through my body -
Like oceans love the earth
With tidal waves
And hurricanes…

I never told you
How I felt for you
Because I felt for you
Through my own suffering -
Like Earth sorrows for people
With its earthquakes
And volcanos.

I will always cry for you
Through my laughter
With someone else -
Because you left me
Before I could ever have
Left you…

BORROWED FEAR

Am I afraid to love you
Because I am afraid to love?

I borrow your eyes
For my starless nights,
I borrow your hair
For the seaweed of my dreams,
I borrow your lips
For whispering of drowning waves,
I borrow your fingertips
For the pebbles of my islands -
I borrow your silence -
For my stormy mind -
But I do not touch your heart;
My love would hurt us both
And I am afraid
Of hurting.

Yet I am afraid of losing you
Because I am afraid of losing.

So I will give you all the stars
I barely guess,
So I will give you all the fish
I catch in dreams,
So I will give you all the winds
Of wavy consciousness
Sweeping over islands
Of my self-esteem,
This I share with you
To dispel your own
Fears -
For a single gleam
Of love.

THROUGH THE SENSES

I feel you in my room of senses,
Lonely as it is,
I feel you within remote chances,
Reeling in my daytime dreams,
Yet senseless is the feeling
                unfulfilled:
Your haunting presence seems to
Elude me through all life.

I feel your strife for love
In all four corners of my room,
Yet, who is counting corners:
Limits of the spirit -
Un-rounded by time -
Posing as a man?

When I count my blessings
I feel your presence with my eyes
And hear the seeing of your voice
Deep within my soul -
Yet do not have you whole;
I do not taste your lips of passion
I do not smell your scent of sex:

Hexed are years of constant waiting
Flexing muscles of my lust.
Lasting love is dating angels;
Humans seem to starve so fast.

Now I feel you in four corners -
Now I miss you with my touch
In the centre of your being.
Fleeing through your body's centre
I try to enter *love!*

VERTICAL EXCERPT

Where are you,
My woman of this world -
The world of disguised needs
Of substitutes of gods?
Will I recognize you now -
When then has failed to last
                till now
And now will never turn
                to future?
Will I recognize you ever?
And if I do - what will I see
Through your human face?

BIRDS NESTING IN THE FOG

My feelings are like
Birds nesting
In the fog - and
Somewhere, there is love -
But it is lacking
Intimacy
Of the soul kind.
I buy the time
To build my nest -
But every straw starts
To feel like the last one...
And time is free -
And time is not -
Only fog remains -
And the birds who are...
will disappear
With time.

DISAPPEARING RAINBOW

Your love feels like the rainbow
Reflecting all the colours
Of potential light:
A beautiful display
Of the incongruent contrast
Of weather extremes -
Insubstantial - somewhere - out there
But unreachable
By human power -
Always staying the same
                distance away
No mater how much I long to
Approach.
Is it the rainbow's fault?
Or God's?
So I would like to thank you,
                my darling
For at least seeing the rainbow
Of our love -
Even though it sadly happened
Merely in my vision.

WATER

You are like water
Running through
My fingers:
Forever changing
Your shape -
Yet same
In principle.
Hot one day,
Could the next -
Yet uninvolved
In heat exchange.
Smooth to touch,
Or full of turbulence -
Yet expressionless
When gone.
Colourless
Like water,
Tasteless -
Despite flavouring -
Water I need -
Yet can never retain.

COLLATERAL LOVE

It is hard to love you
When my headache comes
When you do not…
It is hard to love you
When you say the sun
Does not shine
When it does…
It is hard to love you
When I think I will not
Need more loving
When I will.
It is hard to love you
When you steal away
My hope
From your dream…
But I still love you
By not loving you more
Than you need -
And you will love me
More
When I feed
On someone else's love.

STONE

I am the water of possibility.
You made quite a splash
On my surface -
Rippling me with your
Sudden physical love -
As if you were a stone
Throwing yourself into me -
As if I was your lily pond
You have found
In your accidental forest,
While zooming on
The concrete pavements
Of stone world
Of negative beliefs.
But I am vertical in my depth;
I can barely glimpse
With my soul…
I do not have a bottom
With stones lying there.
My possibility is always bigger.

I tried to retain you
In your fall through me -
And while your stone
Is looking for my bottom
To rest assured -
My web of feelings
Is too fine for a
Passing stone
To even slow it down.
Not even you can help it:
The water cannot
Retain a stone;
It is the bottom
Who does.
But I am bottomless
In both directions -
While you tried to sink
Only one way.

13 SHADES OF HOPE

My thirteen shades of hope
Have the colours of a
Non-existent rainbow,
My thirteen shades of hope
Are windows to my
Missing home…

My thirteen shades of hope
Will make up months
In my every year
I dreamt through,
My thirteen shades of hope
Are Christmas carols
I never sang for you…

I cannot have you in my palms of
                                    feelings -
Because my palms of feelings
Are scooping fallen leaves of yesterday
                                    dreams
And sparkle weak
With the moon-dust of an emptiness
Of the lovers' night
When there is only one left -
So I cannot have you *ever*
In my palms of feelings -
And I cannot hug you
With my arms of crying -
Since my arms of crying
Are groping through the ocean depth
Of all my fallen tears -
And the seaweed of some purpose
Of my devotion of love
Is now but torn and loose, and frozen
In the polar ice of our daily
Sanity -
So I cannot hug you *ever*
With my arms of crying…

And I cannot hold you in my heart of
                                    need
Because my heart of need is bigger
Than my need for life
So I feel only lost in its very vastness

Praying mostly for some love
With my feeling palms
Used for touching shapes of hope-
But real love just does not come
Through open spaces between people
Who must remain free that way -
So I cannot hold you *ever*
In my heart of need…
All you may, or may not, notice
Is my caress-like smile upon your soul
A smile made of my crying
With my palms of feelings
In my heart of need.

With it, I will leave you
Profoundly alone -
Because even you cannot *ever*
Keep me long in your mind
Of puzzlement.

SCALES OF LOVE

Is my sky
The limit
For your
Low-flying love?

If so,
I should crawl
With you
Down to earth
Of possibilities
You may take
For granted -
Like my poems -
But at least
You do take them.
And if I do crawl -
Will I be
A wounded lion,
Or a hopping
Chickadee?
Will we be
Under-the-table
Lovers -
Or under-the-bed
Friends?

TORTURE

The sunshine
Is a subtle torture:
It exists in the flowers and trees
But does not exist in me;
I am on my own.
The stars
Are also a subtle torture:
They exist in the universe of time -
But would not give me place
To exist free.
And the love of people
Is the most subtle torture of them all:
It exists in their need for God -
Yet you cannot shed their needs
In your own and tortured love.

EXCERPT 1

What is the station
Broadcasting love,
What is the frequency,
What is the time,
Where to get receivers
With all of the specs
Beyond the hum-drum
Of everyday drag?
Is there such muting
To suppress the hiss
Of pertinent emotions
Throughout the scale?
We always fail
To broadcast
Love back!

EXCERPT 2

Most likely
I will meet you
In a garden
Of blooming pity -
Where all the roses
Are paper-mache
Elegance of conventions -
And where
Your Valentine heart
Will forever play
Peekaboo with love,
Seeding your own blues
Of puzzlement of life.

OMELETTE & UNIVERSE

When my brain is not
'sunny-side-up'
And rather resembles
An overcooked
'Western Omelette'
I reach for the
Orange juice of sun
And drink you with my eyes
As my joy of senses -
So my soul can feel
A reminder of love
In the universe…

FROG'S QUEST

I am searching
For a cloud of doubt
In the penetrating blue
Of your eyes -
And your face remains
As Sphinx of mystery
Where future
May not happen -
Because of the past!
Will you touch
A frog -
If you know
There is no 'Prince Charming'?

ONLY A WOMAN

(Warning:
Written on a very cold day
Of the heart
When the soul wanted
To take your hand
And fly away
From reason…)

Shiveringly cold
Are some days without you
When all it's true
Is absence of your hug -
A tug at a crying heart;
How could I be
Part of love
When summer would not start
In winter!?
And splinters of the sun
Are everyone's old dream.
How could I beam
Your warmth
And promise of your eyes
When you yourself -
Are only a woman
In dire need of paradise?!

LOVE EGG

Distant ebbs of cry
Are way behind the mountains
Of daily survivor of logic -
So far and high they are
That no two birds
Of soaring
Can fly there,
Anymore.

There was once a door
To happiness of glimpses
With a little girl's love
Peeking through
Her Chinese eyes.

No one cries by now -
Her mother shut the door.
Sweetest tales of love
Are never made like this.
The loneliness of man
Is God's own implied curse
And happiness is ocean
Of the starting verse!

TIME LOOP

In a tiger's paw
A pearl of the Orient
Opened in a lotus bloom -
Soon to be plucked
By the Western wind;
The tiger turned into stone
In his mid-leap
Toward the sun
And the pearls were gone,
Spilled on sandy beaches,
Turning red and beyond reach
Of the sunsets, intended for lovers...
Gentle waves washed over
The tiger's path,
All the footprints
Dissolved in the flow of time
And others found more lotus leaves -
Only without blooms sublime!

HONG KONG SUNSETS

Who would tell winter flowers
On tropical trees - just remembered
When breeze touches your face
Unexpectedly fragrant...

Who would guess steel glass spires
When grass lays down with the wind
To dissipate in calm, just felt
Unexpectedly longing...

Who would see crimson oceans
In the streets expanding with traffic
When heartbeat cannot keep pace
With memories of youth, now fading.

It is only a hint of places
Once perceived as second home -
When there is no first home left -
It is only time loops, my friend,
It is only a theft of consciousness -
And soon no time loops
Will be looping!

SELF-REFLECTING PRISM

The palm tree breezes into a moment
When love remains mostly unknown
On the other side of lonely heartbeats
Just beyond the reflection of tears -
Where spreading chopsticks
Turn into her slender legs
And her revealed centre
Transforms into colours
Of a butterfly
With wings soaking
Tropical sunbeams
In their softness -
Escaping up
Through the rainbow arches
Of unspoken promises -
On a verge of ecstasy,
Where a simple touch
Of reality fingers
Collapses the vision
Into dreams
Already fast forgotten
With a sleeper washed up
On a beach of nothing -
Next to now
And born.

ONLY A HINT

My beach to infinity
Is lonely with desire - yet calm,
With only a hint of birds,
With only a hint of sunrise,
With only a glimpse
Of the promised woman
Who used to live in
My dream of senses -
A dream so senselessly lost,
Yet not forgotten - ever -
Since forever goes the beach
With nibbling waves
              of nothingness
With only a hint of light and bliss
As home.

CINDER BEACH

Welcome to my cinder beach
At the sea of Nothingness.
The waves of days
Go rushing,
Washing the skeleton of land -
The land of something -
Be it only cinder;
It will soon turn rich
Into splendour of a mosaic
Of long collected beauty.

All those countless Selves
You have gone through
                  in cosmic ages
Up to here and now
Do really count.
What a treat -

I am elevating you
                  to delight now
You, who use the imagery
                  of hope -
While your present
                  props of faith
Feel worn out through your
                  frequent needs.

My trick is honest:
I am elevating you to a set of props
So subtle in your mind -
That you will find a single quiver
                  of your thought
Might turn them real
By walking out on them
Forever.

JULY

July in the inner eyes
Of my only love
Is full of comfort meadows
Where no one has to try
To prove the summer skies
And submerge in the lakes
        of autumn
To continue the song of life
Through winter world
        of death.

I MISS YOU

Do I find you
In my yesterday tear
Reflecting my future
Which is now -
Or do I miss you
All somehow,
In all the times,
In all my lives,
In all God's fumbling
For His Paradise?

PREDICAMENT

Your name vibrates in my senses
With a powerful ground state of
        existence
As if you were the hidden essence of
        the universe
With its gravitation
Reaching beyond time and space
To suggest unity with purpose
- so a question returns in my mind:
Am I supposed to liberate your soul
Through the discharge of chemistry
Of our human lives,
Clenching into a spasm of need -
Or should I just love you
In my feelings and memories,
Sadly and privately,
Letting go off all the moisture
Of storms of youth
In favour of dry balmy weather
Of slow retired seasons?

SEASON

You sound so good -
Like a Christmas story would
To children's dreamy eyes
Living on toys and lullabies -
That I wished to be a child -
But I am not.

You smile so warm -
Like full summer giving charm
To fishermen and sailors
With boats and tents, and trailers -
That I wished to be like them
But I am not.

And you touch a lot -
Like a palm tree with its palm
Touches sunsets through the calm
Of hot breezes of the South -
That my mouth would tend
To whisper
The tranquil joy beyond your name -
But I do not.

My silence is to blame
Where mind can skip its shameless
        game
Of reason;
I have my own season
Of Joy.

WISHES

Irrevocably comprised evanescence
Of a Season-to-be-jolly, or not so -
Yet inscrutably inferred essence
To behold, or not quite -
With all my love
Just lingering forcefully into time
Emanating and being, nevertheless...

YOU HOLD ME TENDERLY

You hold me tenderly
In your hands of caring,
Trying to relive my inner pain -
But my pain is stuck inside
After centuries of fight
Of my single life…

You hold me tenderly
In your hands of love,
Trying to mobilize
The universe of Self -
But my Self has collapsed
Upon itself
And gravity is so great
No light escapes.

You hold me tenderly
In your hands of hope.
Wishing for my spirit
To be stronger than it is -
But my spirit is not
Strong enough
To even thank you properly.

INDEFINABLE

The indefinable part of you
Is defying my definition
Of love - the way it saturates,
The way it crusts within,
The way it deftly
Defuses my awareness
Beyond ego's defences
Of self -
I am it - yet I am defied
By myself;
The indefinable of me
Is yours
Beyond any definitions -
But it is also universe's,
It is the content of the void
After love
Crystallizes out
And beyond
Any definition
As the only existence
Ever definable
To itself
Who is total,
Free,
And
Indefinable!

ARIZONA SONG

Grand Canyon mist
Braids your wishful dreams
At sundown -
Grand Canyon bird
Takes your floating thoughts
Along...
Grand Canyon gorge
Whispers in my silent
Conscience -
Deep river flow
Hums into my sleep
Its song.

Dark ancient caves will try
To invite me to hiding there -
But it is hardly fair:
I cannot hide...

Grand Canyon mist
Wipes your loving hopes
At sunrise -
Grand Canyon bird
Left without a single hint -
Grand Canyon gorge
Yawns with boredom
At my sorrow.
You were to me
Much more
Than you ever seemed.

WISHING

Wishing upon love
Is like mere chasing
Morning mist;
You will always miss
A sky-bird chasing
Shades of blue.

Hoping that
Your love is true
Means you hope
You are strong;
When things
Go wrong
All that is
Left behind
Is you.

BROKEN HEART

Cold is the moon
When my heart is in pieces,
Dark is the night
When my soul is blind;
Lead me to light
If your warmth is tender,
Show me the stars
If your eyes see hope.

Cold is the space
When my faith is shattered,
Dark is the mind
When kindness is gone;
You will have won
If you will remember
That your own heart
Is a meeting place!

Here are the pieces
Of my heart:
Put them together
And they will spell
I love you!

WEDDING

From the glitter on the lake
I will extract sunshine flakes
And melt them down to gold:
To make my ring for you,
My bride!
Then I will hold the sky up high
To let you cut out all the blue
From behind the clouds
To help you make a dress to wear
On our wedding day...

All the trees
Will sway in breeze
And symphonies
Will bloom in meadows.
Will we only live in shadows
Knowing well that I have tried...?

Out of shadows evening comes
And moonlight crystallizes air.
There I will make you pelerine
Out of satin night
Studded all with diamonds
Made of countless stars...

The honey-moon will shine for us;
The universe is ours.

FUTURE LIFE

It happened in my future life...
The sky was beautiful like light blue
                              thought -
Whatever colour it was
That became conventional for the sky -
                              (was it Earth?)
And the sun was warm like a smile.
After centuries of twisted existence
People became creatures of love...
(or were not they people any more?)
And among the lovely females of my
                              world (then)
I knew I recognized you - from the past:
Our painful past
When we were
Husband and wife, once
And failed at our human needs...
Now we cherished the polarity of
                              feelings
In sharing
         (was it still sex?)
As if gods within us chose to love
Each other freely -
Like flowers get born inside stars...

It happened in my future life
And it never ended...

HARVEST

I can follow you
In a butterfly
I can sense you
In a dragon fly
I can love you
Up to a rainbow
But how far
Can I go
Before the destination
Of you disappears
In my mind
And I would find
That the dandelions
In my hand died
Before their harvest?

THORN

There is love
In an uncut diamond -
There is love
In an unformed pearl -
There is love
In unheard music -
And all the unsung songs.

There is love
In an un-grown seedling -
There is love
In a starting fruit;
There is love
In a dream of loving
When the lover
Has not come.

There is love
In wilting roses -
There *was* love
In a hurting thorn.

LUNAR SLUMP

A lone dog's howling night
Bites the moon around like bone,
Howling for the master's hand -
Yet the master's heart cries louder,
Crying for his own true mate
Not yet to be found - in Now
Where two stars may cross
                    or not...

If you cut the night cry
Of the lone dog's throat
Would an invisible hawk
Sweep it into the sky?
Would then life just ooze
In the darkened grass
Warming impersonal shadows
With its dark dew of red?

What happened to meadows
Where butterflies once flew?
What is God's flower substitute
For the death of howling love?
Are dog's masters to be starved
For their loss of reason?

It is the blood season of the full moon
Where no angel sings!

SLIVERS

Slivers of sleep
Slip by your net
      of senses
Like tiny silver fish
Shimmering through
Seaweed of your reality,
Too deep
To sustain
Atmospheric
Pressure
Of awakening -
Until your
Awakening falls asleep
In a world of flood...

TOLL OF TIME

Where is she -
Who could have loved me
Through my open palms,
My orange kisses and peace
Beyond a silent song
Of soul?

The toll of time
Has carried her away -
Where breezes go
To sleep
In timid birches
And tender enveloping
Willow trees,
Just above a frozen lake -
Where centuries of love
Had forgotten
To grow.

FUTURE RAINBOW

You became a rainbow
To my rainy cries
(after my old cloudy marriage).
Through your eyes
The sun tried reaching
For my soul,
Yet I failed to open to its warmth.
I failed to have a goal
Close enough to yours.
Through your tender touch
The whole blue endless sky
With subtle breezes of true space
Was giving me a chance
For joy and laughter
Of free birds -
Yet I failed to see it with my
                hurts
        still deep in me...
with my body,
        hungry for the earth,
through your voice -
        so pure and real...
The ocean surf of future
Was rushing to my life
To rejoice with you -
              in hope -
Yet I failed to cope
With the simple presence
        of our precious night
And let you walk away
            from me...
Yet you will always be
My cosmic lover
        somewhere down the road
Of many lives to come -
And the sun will shine
Through our love anew -
        for you to be
A beautiful rainbow
To a humble soul of mine!

I USED TO BE

I used to be scared
Of the height of the sun
When there were women
Basking in it
And I had none of them.

I used to be scared
Of the joy of laughter
When invitation of love
I was after was going
To others - not me.

I used to be scared
Of my future lives
When the present living
With my wife went lifeless
Before you happened to me;

I used to be...
But I am not - any more.

POETRY

I have written
Hundreds of poems
And they took off
Like some lost loose kites,
Or they shattered down
Like broken glass -
Never bringing love across.

I got used to loss of love
- almost -
Since buds of hope
Were nipped by frost
And fruits were scarce
In fall.

I would like to give you all
My poems ever written
From my heart -
Since only who will
Love me back
Shall deserve any
Of the words.

I will start to turn them real
For you and me
To live - not just read -
So look into my eyes
And leave behind
The past on paper;
The benefit is touchable -
The seed of love is us.

LIMITS

By learning
The apparent limits
Of love of our lovers -
We learn our present
Perceived limits
Of our own love,
Or the lack of it.

WITHOUT A CHASE

...but when you come back
The moon will be at its full -
So the roundness of its light
Will roll over our bodies
                    like silver waves -

And when you come back
The rainbow will evaporate up
In our cloudless minds -
So the golden rays
Will re-create our sunny grace.

So when you come back
The restless time of our waiting
Will turn into a timeless now
And we will be making lovers' play:
Love and life without a chase...
So let us embrace
And stay that way
At any distance -
From now on!
You will be never gone.

DILEMMA

Yet now I am returning
To you - before
You would have come back;
Trying to touch you inside
Your consciousness - before
The blizzard breaks my windows,
I am hoping
To kill my feelings! -
Because you do not hear,
You do not answer,
You are not there
(for anyone?).

I touched you so many times
Within so few days -
You were the only woman
In my life with the ways
Of lovemaking -
With intensity of fire!
My grasping senses needed that,
Yet I did not touch you -
In your soul -
Not at all -
Only the blizzard
And then the fire
Are here...

SUBTLE FIRES

TENDER FIRE

Love me teasingly
By giving me
Your liquid flower
On your lace -
While I will trace
Your lips
With tenderness
Of fire...

INNOCENCE

You love the love in me
While I am absorbed in the sea
Of your silent space
Where female sensuality
Is going to embrace
The innocence of little girl's
Big surge for the butterflies -
While 'birds & bees'
Are lurking in your eyes
With your face still solemnly
Directed to God
And the lace of your panties
Turning wet, in accord with health.

INTOXICATION

You sweetly intoxicated my mind
              with your voice -
              so feminine
I could not dissolve
              into my sleep that night;
I lingered with it - over and over -
As much as it lingered with me...

Your voice flowing like a glitter
              on a stream
As if a dream was suddenly
              touching my future days
              with softest shapes
              of things to come -
As if a forgotten feeling
              started returning ever so slowly,
              as to become unreachable
              with a touch of mystery.

Your voice with mellow curves
              of temptation
              and ponds of magic
To torture the body within the mind...
Your voice to find!
Oh God - I need more than your voice!

SOMBRE MOON

The sombre moon
Lights my void sleep -
Cool and resonant
On the petals of senses
Borrowed from Nature
               of love -
And your vermilion robe
Of tender parts of you
Slips into the night -
As if your undernourished
               soul
Was naked for the first time.

The slaughter-house
Of my trapping thoughts
Bleeds all human juices
Into cups of angels
Who stopped drinking them
Long, long time ago -
Because of an indigestion
Of occasional gods.

CHOSEN FREQUENCY

When I was sorting out
The frequencies of beauty
Of the light -
You just came by,
Riding the sunrays of spring -
Like a virgin of dreams,
Yet with your palms
Spread
To meet the fingers of a man
In a passionate grip -
And I suddenly
Chose the very frequency
Of your ray -
Radiating from your
Womanly centre of gravity,
Where all men
Gravitate -
And let your radiance
Expose me thoroughly,
While trajectories
Of our desire
Coincided into
Delight.

FLOW OF CONSCIOUSNESS

Through the game of touch
You became
               my flow of consciousness -
Outside the time
And beyond a touch of a game -
You became the flow of consciousness
                              suddenly
                              exposed
               by your nakedness
Into a brilliant surprise of beauty -
You became my consciousness
With your body projected close to me
Between never and always,
While I stayed everywhere
               at your fingertips
And even closer
               in your mind
               of feelings.
I know,
          I became your consciousness
                    for a moment now
And you became a forgotten dream to
               me
Unbelievably coming true
With your eyes wide open
And inviting tongue -
While your whiteness moved
Through the swirling motion
Of cosmic angels
               living on climaxes,
Being a baby-butterfly-woman
Spreading and closing
Opening and absorbing,
               vibrating!
               exposing -
And embracing your own existence -
Multiplied by two.

THE BOY

As green as the miracle
Of life
Starting with the dark green moss
Under our bare feet of lust -
All the way to thrusting pines
And swaying birches,
All the way to meadow's reaches -
All the way to palm trees
Spreading to the sun
I am the one
Who will worship light
In our flights of love,
Who will starve
My fear
In the presence
Of your hope...
The scope of calm
Can incorporate joy; -
Discover the boy
With his open palm!

WHEN

When you showed me
Your 'petals & bees'
I felt like harvesting
Your sweetest honey
With a kiss of passion.

When you gave me
Your 'strawberries & wine'
I felt you were mine -
Yet free in any fashion.

When I bent you
On the crescent moon
You were giving me
Your gift of sharing.

When I lent you
Tears and joy, my gloom -
You were daring -
Loving me...
And I was wearing
Openly your love.

LITTLE HEAVENS

When I trace
Your triggered dew
With my probing fingers -
My tree of passion
Starts to grow
To precipitate storm...
When the horn
Of calling angels
Heralds bliss
Of Little Heavens -
I am born anew
To share all this
With you!

CRITICAL MASS

After Little Heavens
Opened for us and closed again -
You keep your beating heart
Open wide
For the chain reaction of love,
Where I provided
The critical mass
Of uncritical acceptance
Of the game of higher purpose -
And you provided
The laws of fission
For the same -
To let us sing refrains
Of reasons
For loving without pain...
At those times
When the dawn would cast aside
The fog -
And the rain will unfold pigeons
In the sky of blue...

KEY

You do help me
Hand-polish my key
To your Little Heaven,
Opening for you -
So we can enter together -
And through our passion
Loving every single minute of it,
Loving now each other
In the truest sense of love.

HIGHER OCTAVES

I will take the cords
Of your touches
From your fingers
And your hips
And apply them
To the beat
Of my body's heat
With the underlying
Melody
Of your undulation,
While the ocean
Of your eyes
Will ripple
With the
        higher octaves
Of our passion shared -
And your sighs
        unheard
By many -
Will reverberate
Through my registers
Of feelings,
While the healing
Of our hearts
Will let our souls
Go free of pain.
Our domain of love
Is here and now -
While our Source
        is true -
Always.

PEBBLE

Like a pebble
In my hand
You contain
The roundness
Of your soul,
Preserving it
For my eyes to see,
For my hands to touch
And lustful mind
To eat.

Like a pebble
On my beach
You will contain
Universe
And reach
Our God
Of love
Deep within
Our
Surf.

PEBBLES

Pebbles of your touches
Make my soul go round -
Pebbles on the ground,
Pebbles in the sky -
Rivers running
Underground,
Rivers running high -
Rivers rolling
Through your pebbles,
Through your moans
And through your sighs,
Rivers flowing
Through your fingers -
Pebble touches
Of your thighs -
Undulating river
Rushes over sands
Of dried-up-cries,
Flying rivers
Full of moisture:

Patterns revealed
In the skies,
Sinking rivers
Full of meaning
Invisible to your eyes,
Yet always ready
With their currents…
If you touch the flow of sand
If you touch the land of pebbles
Ends will revive beginnings -
Beginnings so full of patterns
Only your mind sometimes brings
For your pebbles of your feelings,
Flying high with rushing winds -
Running rivers - skies of thunder
Opening the space with wings.
Redeeming the pebbles for you
With so many, many things
Of wonder!

APPRENTICE ANGEL

Thank you darling
For sharing with me my very tip
Of unreleased love -
Since it is in me,
Still smouldering -
As if centuries
Of sweetest suffering
In the arms of karmic women
Lead me toward you again -
As my mistress of God,
And the goddess of lurking lust,
And a sophisticated lady
Of the fast contemporary mind -
As a pure soul
Of apprentice angel -
All that on purpose
To share with me
Your own smouldering tip -
Where the waves
Of your thawing feelings
Originate and end
On their own accord -
Through your own
Unreleased love patterns,
Waiting within you
For a lucky man
(or god) - to be celebrated fully.

WILD FLOWER BUTTERFLY

I want you to be
As free as a butterfly -
A wild flower butterfly,
A free spirited woman -
Yet loving me, nevertheless -
And I will stress
My love for you
As celebration of our
Confluence of souls -
Since I will love you never-the-less
Than a priestess of the sacred love,
The love you can bring in whole
              to men
In dreams and in your arms -
With kisses floating
As some bolts of warmth
            and energy -
With outstretched palms
And flying legs
Like wings of passion,
Inducing wet synergy
            of gliding,
Yet I am finding flower
            transformation
In the meadow of my mind.
Let me also find your eyes there -
In the dewy diamonds of the sun.

GIFTS

I want to see
The splendours
Of your body
And nourish senses
Through your food.
They are splendours
By the virtue
Of my lust -
Which elevates you
From mere
Chemistry of earth -
To creations
Of wonder,
Through which love
Will find
Its grapevine
Of the soul -
Climbing to the spirit
In full sun…
And that is but one
Of many virtues -
I should realize
As gifts!

STAIRS

Will you build
Our stairs of passion
In the name of transcendence
Of our human time? -
Claiming our own consciousness
In the name of heart and lust,
Trusting stars forever rising
In our present now?
Do not make any vows!
That belongs to humans.
Ours are flowers of the void -
Alien flowers
You saw in my eyes -
Even before I was born.
So brace the karmic storm
With calm!
You have me in your palm -
I love you.

FLIGHT OF LOVING FANCY

In our flame
The essence of your passion burns
With eyes of coal;
I do want you whole
In the holy nakedness
Of your human need -
We can both find joy
In the flow of light
Emanating from our dream
Of the universal law
Of One -
Whom *two* would make!

SPIRITUAL FLIGHT

I will send your eyes
To paradise
While praying
To your thighs
My nightly
Passion prayer
Of our love,
Tasting the moisture
Of your midnight rose -
And playing the strings
Of your golden harp
Of sacred lust -
Tuning it with a single key
Of your budding nakedness
Where your sensations
                go wild -
Like flowers in a storm
Of summer heat -
And then I fit my stem
Of joyous rising
To your dimension of need
To accomplish our abyss
Of spiritual flight
Into a rebirth of pure light
In our humble souls!

WILD WHITE BIRD

In the bedroom
Of your heart
I want to love your soul
As a wild white bird
Soars the mountains
For the whole blue sky...

In the bedroom
Of your heart
I want to find your light
To elevate my dark of longing
With clawing lust
To hook your soul
And stroll in naked gardens
Of our dream...

And if your loving quit
I would soothe your thighs
With my angel wings
Spreading them apart -
Bringing all the things to light
In the bedroom of your heart.

WORSHIP

I rested, lying supine
On a rock beside the ocean
When you came to lie with me.

You - the wave of salty air
With your hair spread
By water like a sea anemone.

You simply touched my shoulders
So I stayed that way
And you lay on me.

I stretched my arms to let
The sun and you work
The worship - all astride.

And you tried to be
The best of priestesses.

SCULPTOR

When your living flower
Opens for my love -
I would starve my hunger
Half the way to heaven -
Just to see you bloom,
While carving petals
With my tongue.

MELON

You cut a juicy melon
Open - on your lap,
Offering me a summer treat
Beyond my dreams -
And when you unfolded
Its fragrant meat
- separating seeds from fruit
For my benefit -
I could not resist
Thirst and hunger
For your sudden gift -
And took the plunge to eat,
And drink,
And swallow juice
With abandon and free.

Your hips were crushing
Straw-mats underneath
And the summer itself
Had an open melon
For the sun -
Slowly falling…
I was feasting at your feet
And calm was calling stars
To cover us with night,
While our love was roaming
Freely through our dreams.

IMAGE

You
Braided daisies
In your hair
Where your pubic
Lips wait silent -
You invited me
To your island
With your fruits
To share -
With your moon eyes
Full of hint,
Dancing to me
With the wind…

GENTLE WIND

In the gentle mist
Of the summer woods
I would seek your touch
Through the beams of light…

I would hope I might
Slide alongside your body
With my throbbing need
To have you there - and quick -

…and then you would pick
                    a clearing,
Undressing so silent -
And let the wind go
Through your fingers,
Caressing your breasts
And belly, going round
                    your hips - -

So let the wind now kiss you
With a petal touch -
Right in the centre
Of your womanhood -
All on my behalf
And for your good,
My woman!

SUN WORSHIP

In the sunlight
Where so many other flowers
Bathed and swam just before you -
In the sunlight
Saturated with the fragrant dew -
You are taking a bath now.
You - a flower prettier
Than summer dreams,
More alive and lovelier
Than pouring golden beams -
And you have let me watch you,
Being caressed by the sun -
And you have let me count
        your petals -
     one by one,
      over and over,
Finding the ends
In the beginning of our love.

DANDELION SUMMER

My eyes were tired
Like drying puddles
After the yesterday's cry,
While high in the blue
Of the sky of my mind -
There was a rotating ball of joy
Still without a name.
When I looked into
A green grass around me,
Just after it had had its haircut,
There was still one dandelion left;
It was enough sun
For the rest of the day.

Next day you took me in the meadow.
Many tiny smiling suns
Were inviting us to lie down…
…and when you hugged your legs
Behind my back,
One of the dandelions
Turned into a yellow butterfly
Who tracked the sun
Way to your own
Smouldering warm
Fuzzy ball
Of joy.

IN THE MIDDLE

In the middle of my night
I let my flight of fancy
Guide my need to dare -
Being free to share my love,
Lying, sleeping next to you -
Trying a thing or two
To reverberate passion's heat -
Letting you soon benefit
From being a woman.

51

VOLCANO

A staccato of my heartbeat
Would wake me up
In the middle of my night,
Speeding in a hot anticipation
Of finding you next to me
With your little moans of pleasure
Rolling down your pillow
In the rhythm of your gentle fingers
Ever so slowly circling under your
                              blanket -

Feeding your own responses
Into a focus of the heat -
Causing me to freeze
In order
Not to disturb you too soon -

While soaking in all your heat waves
Of undulating motion of your hips,
Feeding myself on your
Beautiful hunger

And your wholesome
Mature acknowledgement of it
In a creative action
Beyond any dream -
Then I would release a built-up stream
Of rushing monsoon rivers
In sweeping countryside
Of explosion of flowers
Joining you in your flight
To steepest volcanos
Of passion -
High above the clouds -
Where the space is penetrated
Into the sheer motherhood
Of belonging to nature -
And where our liberated bodies
Will let our souls find
Purity of songs
Of the very coming dawn
Of life!

SOUL ASYMPTOTES

TALL ORDER

My evening star
Became a self-imposed
Illusion -
The primordial truth
That remains
Quietly virtual
In the messed-up
Reality
Of a defunct ego.

So the calm pervades
All the turbulence
Of pain -
And sanity
Is but a strain
Of existence -
But not fully Being.

I am seeing
Without looking through,
But I cannot see
My clue
Before looking up
And seeing all …

(Tall order, isn't it?)

HUMAN RACE

He came to his world
With weeping ponds
Of hushed light quasars,
With empty fistfuls
Of stardust lost -
With love that costs
All centuries of lifetimes
And sometimes more
Than one can
Humanly still bear…

He came to dare -
And love just
Danced itself to stardom,
Stormed-out through
The nights of pain -
Quite insane -
With needs of human
And goals untold
In bold of space - .
He turned his face
To inner music
And put his needs
On hold -
Permanently;
He just ceased to be
Of human race.

PREMATURE ENLIGHTENMENT

How do you boil the stone?

You just let the pebbles
Bubble in the liquid sun
And stoically stun the boulders
Into gravel -
So your stony road
To marvellous marble
Of worldly success
Won't get chipped off
By your premature enlightenment -
Until you decide to let the stone
Grow into ground -
Or fly with the birds
In the sky -
So your high aspirations of life
Happen to outlive
Your low asparagus of vegetable soup
You cooked for yourself -
To eat in earthly dignity
Of physical hunger,
While you were dieting
From heavenly desserts
unnecessarily!

MIRROR

I am just a mirror
To other people,
Because they could be
Part of me -
And as such,
I am just
A partial reflection
Of myself with them.
Only if I met
That someone
Who would mirror me
Completely
May I become real
And powerful
Like the light
Of the laser beam.

EARLY AWAKENING

Trinkets of sleepiness
Will shatter and blend
Into the solid state
Of the liquid crystal
Of the sun of love -
Be it only half
The frequency
Of creation
Time will carve
Into our *being* infinite!

CHILDREN

Walking through our gardens
We will be touching
Grown-up trees of passion,
Listening to the music
In our voices -
And caressing the flowers
Of our bliss…
Then we will lie down
In a meadow
Left behind by butterflies -
And become spiritual
Children,
Transcending all this -
Into bliss even higher!

HOW TO FLY

Birds as symbols
Of freedom
And their songs
Could be keys
To our souls.
Sharing enhances
Our opportunity
To perceive the songs
Around us -
And the songs within -
And, therefore,
Enhances our life.
In time -
Life can become
A song to us
And its loving tune
A key to our
Spiritual freedom.
And before you know
How to fly -
You can become
A rainbow butterfly.

THE WAY TO BE

To fly
Without wings
To love
Without a lover
To live
Despite the life;
To be
From inside out -
Not to dream
From outside in!

DESIRE

You feel
My ability to love
And it makes you
Fly.
I feel
Your ability
To love back
And it makes me
Shudder -
While burning
With desire
For both:
Loving
And
Flying!

THE WAY TO FLY

To fly
On wings of soul -
To love
Through
Lover's loving -
To live
While expanding
One's life -
To be
One's source:
Both in and out;
To know
The dream
From outside in!

REALITIES

Echoes of percolating silence
Always seeping through
The words of post-realizations
Of personal realities
Will eventually crystallize
Into an ultimate wisdom
Of love -
Beyond the personal!
… music is, so far,
        the closest …

MUSIC FROM WITHIN

Music from within -
Unfolding its petals
Into a virtual
Flower of lotus -
Like feelings of being
Human, yet infinite
From within, -
Forming tentative
Bloom of potential
From beyond, -
Yet feeling God
Here and now -
Within music!

ARCHITECTURE

Architecture of God
Merges with architecture of man
Enveloped by architecture
Of music -
Which belongs to angels.

RAINBOW

What a symbol
Of forever arching
Spectre of light,
Glorifying the range
Of diversification
Of Godly premise
Toward a poetic abstraction
- come real -
All in the eyes
Of an observer
Who might be
Too awe-struck
With a dewy longing
Around his eyelashes
To really see
        the treasures
At the end
        of the rainbow.

Does the rainbow end
At its end?

RAINBOW VISION

As the heavy clouds rolled by
Leaving just a veil of rain in their wake,
The 'incredible-of-the-sun'
Happened again:
A rainbow!

And so - an illusion of our senses
Re-established itself as our reality
Anew: A view of light!

So why to struggle
To see individual droplets
When the design comes
As a whole!

Final goal of awareness through life
Is to realize the delight
Of playing along with the game
                    of existence;
Since our happiness through its
                        truest sense
Is the only possible score
                with eternity.

And score - we do:
We cannot reach the rainbow
In our silly ways of reaching -
But the rainbow stays in sight,
Teaching us the perception of light.

SHAPES

Mental shapes of beauty -
As unreachable
As a snowflake
On a naked palm...
Mental shapes of beauty -
Less than skin deep,
Torturing the mind's eye
With deep-seated need
For the Absolute;
While
Relative shapes of beauty
Haunt the sleeper
With daylight dreams
Of a possible world -
Where
Mental shapes of beauty
Either become real -
Or transcend
On a beam of light -
So sublime and pure,
That all the shapes
Would become obsolete!

HOW!

How do I long
To make my
Music of love
And populate
New universes
With my children
Of love -
Who would finally
Listen to their
Own music
        of Being -
And practice
Love without fear,
As easily as they
Would breathe
My ongoing energy
Of my loving
        sustenance,
Since I am
Forever alone
In my absolute -
Yet one with you!

APPRENTICESHIP

Who could, nevertheless, decide
When we should love
And when we should not?
Since apprenticeship of love
Never ends
And we love someone ...
Yet someone we do not ...
And the time
Is a mere repetition
Of eternity
For the whole purpose of love
We have not mastered yet.

VERTICAL PROJECTION

On our projected flights
To the nocturnal parts
Of our insightful needs -
You show me your horizon
Of purpose -
Like a focused vortex
To the other universe
We both came from,
Be it by mistake -
Or just looking
For each other... -
In our rather nebulous
Quest for light.
The other universe
Was bright
And horizons were
Vertical:
So full of hanging stars
That sparse was
Only darkness...

POETRY READING

The transcendent beauty
Of the inner quest
For transcendent beauty
Shown in your eyes -
When you read aloud
The flowers of your soul -
And while your whole face
Was structured to resonate
Emotions of humans,
There was a reflection
Of a gentle waterfall
Of shining silence
From the beyond
Of your garden.

The waterfall will remain
Unreachable - for me,
Reaching for you merely
Through your human window -
Even if I loved you
A thousand times...
So I will not.
Some flowers grow
In my garden, too.
Yet the waterfall is one
For both our gardens.
One day we will embrace
In its cascades of pure light
In spirit -
And become love ourselves.
We *all* will.

DIMENSION OF SILENCE

The night
I did not touch you
In the circular
Motion of my heart -
And started non-dreaming
As a choice of the sleepless
Sleep of the mindless part
        of rest -
To effervesce my morning
With a renewed promise
Of a hope - to touch
The paradise of your sharing -
The night after
And the 'ever-after' times;
Lonely chimes make
Waiting music -
But silence knows
Beyond
The human language
Of love.

RENEWAL

The mystery of renewal,
Revealed in a single embrace,
When surrender happens
From within the matrix
Of sacred silence,
Pierced by sun,
Strewn with rocks,
Washed by waves,
And savoured
By our senses -
Will elevate
Our human chances
To a chalice Offering -
Overflowing with Light,
Where delight
Of love's own sharing
Is now beyond
The right or wrong.

Let us be daring:
Let our love grow strong.

HOW TO DRINK

How to drink
Before pouring?

Just realize
The goblet is full
To start with!

*Bottomless **and** full!*

FROM THE FIRST DROP

From the first scribble
To a masterpiece
Soaking wet in soul.

From the first drop
Of sharing
In the daring human needs

To a river of the flow
Where all people
Go to celebrate!

It is never late
To return to the sea
Where all our motion
Meets the calm.

Not for some -
For all of us it works:
From the first drop
To the ocean
Inside everyone!

EMOTION OF STORM

We are the watchers of our spirit -
Psycho-meteorologists
Of our cosmic weekend weather
When our weakness
Culminates to strength
Of pre-storm warnings -
When the emotional fronts
Of high and low
Collide inside holes of time -
When everything is fine
In the eyes of hurricanes,
When we appear sane -
Planning patterns of the flow,
When it is time to go
With our private storms
All the way we came together,
When our space is too tight
For fast lightnings of the light -
But our cosmic station
Gets us back from harm
Right into the eye of the hurricane
Where love elates the being
And seeing transfers
Tornados of calm.

MEADOWS OF MY MIND

There are meadows in your mind
Where no one ever walked
To even glimpse the sunny stretches
Of the groves of birches
In the whispered grass
Of your subconscious…
Mind plays tricks on everyone -
When feelings burst
Like geysers through the desert rocks
To produce rainbows -
Where hawks were only hunting,
Guarding sanity of every silly dream - .
It seems like yesterday:
Our first love inherited from some
                                                angels
Of our cosmic past - is gone -
Or is it here to stay?
How *vast* is timeless moment
Of our gulping search to a single tear -
Full of sacred ponds
Of God's own Paradise…
Could you ever come so near
To see the size of my need -
So silently outgrowing
The human being I am in?
There are meadows of your mind
Your emotions will find for you
Through the worldly prayers of pure
                                                springs
With crystal trickles of the diamond
                                                light
In selfless offering of our daily goals -

I hope to be around - one day
In the essence of the flight
Over the countryside and ponds,
While reminiscing with your past from
                                                within -
Yet never present - only that can last.
I hope to be around
When our future mind will guide us
To understanding - we have been
                                                standing
Side by side for ages - yet ages more to
                                                come…
There are meadows in *my* mind, too!
The time surged through its span
To tie in its beginning there -
So waiting is meaningless
And fair amount of music
Is given to your countless loves…
I am waiting for you there -
In the *distant future* -
So close to God
That our distinctions
Will merge with His;
Yet I am waiting there
Already now -
In a *lost meadow* of my mind!

I NEED YOU LESS

... and I need you less
Since water does not hold
            its scars
And I am approaching
Its fluid state -
As if being sand ...

I need you less
And love you more -
Yet at the distant shore
Of cosmic consequence -
So you may not yet benefit
From my feelings
And flights beyond
In the present tense,
Since even you
Have to spread
            your wings
One day -
To become the wind ...

I need you less
Yet would never lose you -
Only when my need
            is gone.
So I lose you
In this life - -
But losses of this kind
May well count as gains
Out there - at the distant shore
Of cosmic consequence,
Where lovers like us
Are lovers with God.

OCEAN ROCK

Sometimes when I cry
Overtime rain
For the evening sun
Slipping through my fingers -
I feel ocean depth
With emotional tides
Blending black with blue
And silver streaks of wind - while
Gold belongs to sun
Sliding on your hair -
And air belongs to birds
Singing in your soul.
Yet I cannot fly
To touch the time of yours
In my heart - we are apart.
Then
I would trade the depth
For solid calm of stone
And I would find my home
Right next to the ocean.
One day you would come
And find my ocean rock
Stretched long in the sun
To stir up your emotion.
And you would lie in nude
On my warmth of stone,
Feeling distant beat
Of my stony heart.
For that fleeting time
I would be alive
And I would be a part -
Of your tender flesh.
A sparkle of your love
Would sink into my calm
And within thousand years
My rock would grow its depth.

REVERBERATIONS

Mirror of fog -
Thunder of mountains -
Waves upon waves -
Spring, summer, fall -
Barking of dogs - -
Body sound clapping ...
Faces of moonlight
Will not cover all
The reverberations
Of atoms
Of progressions
Of seasons -
Years of climaxes,
Rows upon rows of crosses
And ricocheting Big-Bangs
Throughout eternity
Of every single second
Of God
Will not do -
Only total silence
Will.

EARTH

In the cleavage of time,
You - a creative illusion
Of the creation to be -
The planet Earth -
In the sea of possibilities -
You have become
The becoming of many
Who will turn you real -
Beyond the realm of illusion -
In the process
Of their own transcendence ...

CRYSTALLIZATION

Diamonds in the fallen leaves -
Unclaimed diamonds
Among sunny rubies of the trees,
Scattered diamonds
Of the crusty snow
Blowing softly, crystallizing
                    freezing tears -
Dewy diamonds
Of the muddy growing grass -
Scars-like fractures
                    dissolving in rainbows -
Fears of sharpness
Of the beauty of the diamonds
Of the reflections of light -
Fights of 'Is-ness' in a pool of 'I' -
High and low of harvests
Of the Thanksgiving with dreams,
Un-dreamt or dreamt throughout past
Of years of digging for the diamonds
Where other rocks would roll by
Like some cheerful gears of history
Of man who needs to strive
To achieve peace in giving up at last.
Falling leaves
And rising music,
Strolling memories of past
And dazzling future -
Giving up all diamonds
And getting light
Beyond their form;
Storm is over -
Only songs go
Beyond sunsets,
Only death goes
Beyond dreams.
Streams of consciousness will
                    crystallize
And darkness becomes bright again.

POWER OF LOVE

What makes love
So powerful…?
Is it the ever-increasing
Inner freedom
And security of purpose,
Personally realized through
Broadening of subtle,
Awareness all-underlying
Of spiritual principle
      of existence,
Slowly being structured
In consciousness
With feelings of
      the Indestructible,
God's energy, working toward
The assured balance
Of beauty…?

SACRED LOVE

You will be like ocean:
An unbound woman -
Magical and free,
With a karmic meaning
To my hungry soul.
And I will be your shore:
The goal of waves
Which long for more
Than sandy beaches
And gentle surfs…
You will wash my
      cliffs anew,
Bringing sacred love
Within your wavy motion -
And I will give your deep waters
The gift of light
Which will make us
Whole again!

DYNAMIC PRAYER

One of the dynamic prayers
Through positive action
Will come about
With our fingers, lips and tongues
When we reciprocate
In a flight of passion
Of our singing bodies -
With no doubt
Of the heart within a heart,
Within a hope
Of the soul
To hold on -
On a dream
Of gods -
Since The God
Is becoming
Through us!

DIMENSIONS

The water rests
In the never-ending sways of waves
Like the time stopped still - in now -
And the sun will set and rise
In a mindless glory of the light,
Spiralling through dimensions of man -
Projected to a space-less point
Belonging to angels -
Like the eye of a needle,
The eye of a hurricane,
The eye of God -
Who will remain nameless!

OUR IMAGE

With the untenable tool
Of happiness
We are carving
The face of God -
To our image - -
But the only image
Is God's!

TRANSCENDING GOD

I need to hear your female voice
Before I can make my choice
Hearing the silence of God.

I need to feel your female hands
Before feeling reverence
For countless hands of God.

I need to see your loving face
Before hoping for a place
In front of the face of God.

I need to touch your flowing hair
Before soothing my despair
Not being able to touch my God.

I need to love the whole of you
Before I can become true
Surviving on love of God.

I need to know you want to share
Before I can even dare
Surrendering all my needs to God.

I need to call you tender names
Before I can shed the chains
                    of words
Not having to use the word G o d
                    any longer!

ANTI-ENTROPY

The original God
Of the semantic void
Always pregnant
With fulfillment
Of infinite opportunities
To be more
Through creation
Of derivative Selves...

The original God
Beyond any
Time concepts
Measuring its existence
Through refracted
Experiences of progress
But also through the times
Of His own creation...

The original God,
As the structure
Of the Universe,
As the template
Of the order of orders
Holographicly mirroring
Its crystallography
Of light within Light...

The original God
Has already become
The final God -
Yet - since His Becoming
Is never finished,
Being infinite -
The game of progress
Defies the scope of itself,
Leaving the
                    Anti-entropy
As the only surrogate
Of its Origin.

MINIMAL KARMA

My karma leads me
When it is maximal
And I strive for intensity
In the print-through
        of time,
Inventing my life -
While dying to cradle
My emotions in wombs
        of sharing -
To tuck my
        feelings
In spirit crib of waiting dawns,
Sunrises of silence
In my clamorous mind
To lead my karma gently
When it is minimal,
Yet in hindsight
That is the time
When detached balance
        of my surface calm
Pretends strength of quiescence -
When the essence of my days
Accelerates time -
While my mind has stopped -
Just short of a limbo state of hope
        for non-existence -
Through union with the concept
        of unity with all -
So I am led to fall
When my karma is minimal
Just to rise at other levels
Of my see-saw Self -
And while my leading is
        Maximal,
I minimize my karma
Being overwhelmed and humble,
Putting quiescence on a cosmic shelf.

When we transcend our
Illusion of fulfillment
Through routine pleasures
Of physical
        coincidence,
We may find ourselves walking
In the desert of night
Where cosmic lessons come
Seemingly uninvited
Like stepping stones in the sand

'Til we are exhausted
Crawling at the end -
Yet our spirit seems so still -
Poised before flight -
And while our groping reason
        stretches toward light,
The first glow of dawn's horizon
Is well beyond
        our vision.
Memories go shuddering
Towards the invitation
To wishing for non-being
Where the potential of pain
Is impossible!
But minimal karma is somewhere else
And we have to see
Through the trick of self-awareness:
By longing for mere nothingness
We do long for our karma's end.
So should we send it rolling wild
Or should we transcend it?
We cannot hide from ourselves -
        not for long -
Since the very time is a growing child
Of eternity…
But we are strong! -
And therefore liable.
Karma is long
But I love you now -
And now is forever
If we could give up
The future as fear.
Karma is slow
But I love you fast -
And speed becomes permanency
If we could give up
Change as insecurity.
And karma is strong
But I love you being weak
And acknowledging weakness
Becomes strength
If we could give up
Clinging as safety.
Because only the unknown
Quickens our becoming…
Karma is long
But I love you!

SOUL SEARCHING

You are free
If you realize you are free.
You are free to accept the burden
Even if its name is love -
But you are free not to accept a burden.
You are free to suffer,
Being afraid of suffering,
But you're free not to accept suffering -
If you are not afraid of being free
To sacrifice your fear,
Turning weakness into strength,
But you are free to remain strong
With your weaknesses untouched
      by giving.
You are free to give by giving
      uninvited,
You are free to invite on your own
If you are free enough
Not to wait for invitation
      by others.
And you are free to accept
What is freely given to you,
Providing you are free enough
To remain feeling free
Disregarding the timing of acceptance.
And you are free to miss the timing -
Yet you are free to remain timeless,
Providing time does not scare you
From being free.
You are free to believe
But you are not free to know.
You are free to choose your karma,
Providing your karma is to *be* free.

VERTICAL CONVERGENCE

Some days
I am lonely for the space
Beyond my memories.

I am lonely for the touch
Of vertically floating time,

I am lonely for the distance
Hidden in a point.

Some days
I am lonely for a voice -
I am lonely for the voice
Beyond meaning of words.

I am lonely for the light
Needing no darkness to show up,

I am lonely for myself
Who would be without myself.

And I am lonely for you -
Without you…

But one of these days
I will find out
Inside-out of you
And outside-in
Of everything -

So I will be lonely no more.

PROMISE

I promised my body
Hungry for love
A female body to have.
I promised my soul
Hungry to share
A female soul to care.
How many times
Did I promise
The abundance of existence,
While my existence -
With its lonely hands
Was reminding
My body consequence
Of missing company
Of hope -
To find a female
Who could cope
With spiritual sex!?

A WOMAN ON A ROCK

A woman lying on a rock
Hair draping the clouds -
Prays to sky,
Prays to earth -
A woman on a rock
Arms stretched wide
Embracing stone with her breasts
Prays to flying hawks,
Prays to rising pines -
A woman on a rock
Embracing stone
Claws with fingers in the cracks,
Hugs with hips
The great cold stone -
And holding tight;
Prays to lightening,
Prays to stone,
Stone waiting for fire...
A woman hugging with her hips,
The great rock,
Her body merging
Through spasm -
Prays, while her breasts slowly
intergrow with earth -
Prays while her soul
Intermingles with sky
She prays and prays -
Fingers clawing -
Hips hugging -
A woman on a rock,
With arms stretched wide.
Prays for love
Prays for life.

FINDING SELF

In my subtle quietness
Of a waking dream
I do not dream -
Just let my feelings come
And then - a garden
Merges with the house
Where I compose
Rhapsodies
Of inner balance
Of the joy of truth,
Reshaping the music
Of all seasons -
As if Christmas fireplaces
Warmed me through
The endless calm
Of being finally home -
In the embrace
          of a woman soul
I must find
Before ever finding Self!

TRUTH

So truth for us stays
Multidimensional like waves
Of our searching consciousness
Of the swelling sea of God -
Glistening in the nothingness
With the true
Alien light.

WITH A HUNGRY HEART

One of the vaguely pristine
Fresh and wet mornings
With re-invented birds and trees,
When all one needs
Is a mountain -
To become a Mohammed,
Yet the world has agenda of man
And you are no messenger of God
To the people needing bread.
It is in your head!
(Or is it in your karma?)
With a hungry heart you step
Right into a garden
From beyond!

GLANCE

Between yesterday and tomorrow,
Between one second and the next,
Between your single swallowed tear
And a quiver of hope around your lips -
                    now relaxing in a smile -
I want to touch the child of your soul
                    and call it a present
Before it will turn into eternity,
Changing our elusive existence
Into true existence -
With no mystery of separateness left.

In a cleavage of Absolute
We snuggle for a short, short lifetime
To have a chance...
Let us exchange notes
On everlasting doubts,
Let us glance together
                    at the purpose.

ESTATES OF THE MIND

Estates of the mind are real;
They are more than properties,
They are more than what we feel -
Or imagine as dreams -
They are truly dwelling places
For our souls to grow -
Since we become truly we
Only being home,
Somewhere - some of the time -
Always altering time's flow,
Being altered ourselves.

CITIZENSHIP

I am a traveller -
You are the country,
Country I wanted to reach -
Hoping my currency of values
Was a legal tender there…
I had more than plenty -
More than I thought I had;
I nearly became rich -
And the country on your own
Was more than fair to me.
You accepted my name
And I could plainly see
That even the language here
Was the same as mine:
The country felt like home
Since the pain of existence
Tends to travel in my bag,
Limitations seem to grow
With experienced freedom…
To be home is not to lack
The access to the Source within
And also a bit of love to feed on.
You are resourceful as country
And I am considering
A citizenship status here,
Turning the outer limits
Into freedom from within.

TRAVELLER

I am a traveller,
I am a visiting place!
You visit me like Mecca
Of your hope
On your travels
To happiness.
I visit myself in my mind
To meet with another traveller:
To meet *you*!
To rejoice in countryside
Of mutual awareness
Of freedom to travel,
Yet also freedom
To stay at a visiting place -
Or even to dwell there
For the rest of the trip
Of our human tour.

ENOUGH

I cannot love you enough
To make you exist -
Because of my fear of existing
Without love,
And thus be responsible
For its creation -
Despite the void
Into which
The need for love turns,
When even God
Is to be created within
Your deepest despair,
Just because you need Him -
Since you cannot
Cease to exist
Before you love.

PURIFICATION

I feel like
Extracting hours
From my seconds,
Extracting silence
From my music,
Extracting feelings
From my calm
And feeding them
To light
Extracted from darkness -
Feeding them to love
Extracted from sorrow,
Feeding them to joy unbound -
While extracting
Always from Never
And returning to
Now!

TIDES OF LIFE

When you feel me in your mind
There are tides
Deep inside your body,
Reaching for a touch-down
On an island of hope -
        - a rest within our voyage.

Knowledge of truth,
Coming as trust
Through our surrender to faith,
And bypassing the human fear -
A chase for safety,
Remains without words.

Birds - like thoughts -
Are nesting despite seasons.

Tides of life
Defy all reasons
Rippling through our souls
        and bodies.
When you feel me in your mind
Eventide of human truth
Dawns into the light
Beyond the original Word.

WING

A wing -
Almost touching
The sky ...
Just one wing (!)
The other
Crippled
In the sea of love ...
Not a bird:
Rather
So called
Human ...
Swept away
By the power
Of his existence - ?
Or rising into
Nothingness
Which is all?!

INVISIBLE BIRD

The invisible bird
With a transparent beak
Brought me the memory
Of your sensual sighs,
While my own music
Was still lingering
Within the silence
Of my loneliness.
The untouchable caresses
Of your distant mental fingers
A transient indulgence -
Rolling over my naked body
Like a gentle playful surf -
And beneath me: the warm sand
Of a tropical sunset
Of my unfulfilled romantic vision
Was letting me sink
Into an oblivion of trajectory
Of one of my dreams which are
Unbound by humanity,
Yet are unliveable
On this planet:
I am an alien.

A LOADED DICE OF LIFE

Unreachable you -
Not to speak of
Myself -
Since I am here,
Closer
To the dilemma:
How do you plead:
enlightened or
innocent?

THE POWER

The power of stone
Is encased light
Of waiting -
In the mating season
Of all galaxies ...

The power of love
Is all of this and less
Like when chess is played
To stall -
Since winning
Would just end
The very game!

THE TRUE HOME

The brightest
White light -
As the energy
Of your soul,
As the part
Of the whole
Is your true home
Where forever takes
Every second
Of your single being,
Overflowing
Throughout universes
Of spasms of love.

COSMIC WAITING

I feel them often
But usually far -
Yet I feel them so close
Sometimes,
Just hovering
Above the planet,
Just radiating
Above my consciousness,
Just waiting -
For a contact - ?
Or to make one?

Expectations
Precipitate into desire,
Desire precipitates
Into long sweet longing
And your empty hands
                and mind
Always precipitate
Into the basic
                cosmic waiting -
Waiting through
                the waiting period
Of human time -
Just before a promotion
To beauty ...

CLAIM OF CALM

Now I want to claim - nothing
But your consciousness
Through the night of heat and heart
As I have to claim your love
Through your woman's body
Hiding in an angel ...

As I have to stay insane
Within the many reasons
Of your very God
Who will give you kingdoms
Beyond worlds of mind.

As I have to remain kind
To all poor souls in their need
Full of tender ignorance,
Including mine -
Which was kind enough
To claim my consciousness
In this world ...

If you hear the silence
Of my alien doubt and plight
Will you listen
To my shouts of karmic need,
Containing seeds
Of our future light?

KNOWING

Just to hold you
Through the sacred
Interface of love ...

Just to hold you
Like a tender blossom
Through the meditation
Of my cosmic awe ...

Just to release you again
Through the dissipating
                    diamonds
Of the midnight dew,
Scattering the light
Of the distant stars ...

Just to let you rise
Through all new flowers
Of the loving energy of life,
Kneeling at the subtle touch
Of a Monarch butterfly
In my lustful supplication

To your female essence -
But praying to your soul
For your ascendance in light
To your inner peace
Of knowing my love
From within your own.

CITIZENSHIP (2)

From the soft glow
Around your eyes
One can model universes
Of living landscapes
In the skies of purpose,
Structured
Throughout consciousness
And nourished
With our love,
Where half
Of perfection
Qualifies one
For a citizenship -
While a whole heart
Of human need
Would make one
      a king there.

SUPPLICATION

Whether or not you will be
      my lover again -
You will always be
My beloved of this world,
Disregarding any number
Of wives I have had;
You will be married to me
Through the magic
      of your past -
Since you are
A germinating pearl
Of golden light
Of cosmic equinoxes
Where my calm will give you
Love beyond your doubts
Of this world.
Through my prayer
To your womanhood,
I am elevating you
To gardens from Beyond
Where your future memories
Will have me as your love
Though humble in my limitations
With timeless tenderness
To last you lifetimes
      and linger
In your soul forever.

RECOGNITION

Sometimes
      I can almost taste
My forgotten alien memories
      of yellow-purple skies
Where butterfly flutter
      of joy
      could tunnel itself
      into blissful dives
Of vertical
      sunshine recognition
      of light.

STRANDS OF MEMORIES

I almost remember the skies
Of purple hues
      and yellow sun
When you hummed your
      tune of love -
Mauve reflections
      flickered in your eyes -
While subtle flames
      of static
Charged out from the
      orange strands
Of your moving hair -
Attracting stares
Of stagger-birds of love,
Standing on one leg,
Watching us
      mate -
In the late hour
Of our burning planet
In cosmic transformation
To a higher-level-universe!

How come we are here?

PICNICKING

In a single folding petal
Of a single rose (or orchid)
Slipping within softness,
While emerging in light,
I will discover universes
For our final flight
To our alien home of love!

It was not a rose - I carved for you;
Do you not see the yellow flower
Against purple skies?
Do you not know the ancient
                    word-names
For alien flowers
In your native tongue?
Rolling with the sound of
                    silence
In your silent mind?
Singing always voicelessly
Through the music soul
When you are forever more,
Accepting less,
                    - owning nothing,
In peace gaining everything -
If you follow me in light
When I slip within your
                    softness
Of our purple home -
Picking all the grapes of passion
Of our ancient heritage.

ALIEN FLOWERS

At the boundaries of your sleep,
Or better yet,
At the edge of your visions,
Colours shine through
Members of living species of light
Where you might have started
Growing alien flowers -
Inadvertently dropping your
                    pearly seeds
Among the weeds of angels.
Nobody cuts grass in heaven;
Rewards come in purgatory.
That is for people needing stories -
                    not flowers -
So your wild alien blossoms
Are in fast transit
Between Love and commitment
                    to Earth.

ETERNAL EYES

A real dream
Became even more real
In my dream -
When I sensed your eyes,
When I saw your eyes,
When your eyes
Were the total
Of the dream -
When your eyes
Dissolved my soul
Into tenderness
And safety
Of being-ness -
When I merged
With the ponds
In your eyes
And light which
Engulfed us
Together - in love -
Beyond
Any human limits ...

... so love me, because I am one of the
        women of your God...

... so love me in return, because I am
        one of the men God gave you!

ABOUT THE AUTHOR

Jiri Jirasek was born at the onset of World War II in Czechoslovakia. A gifted child, he started writing poetry and music in his early teens.

During the 1960's, he founded the art photography group, Imaginum, which became a participant in numerous international exhibits and competitions. Though his natural bent was profoundly artistic, he pursued a scientific education and obtained an Engineering degree from Prague University.

In 1968 he established his new home in Canada with his first wife and two children. Though English was his second language, it soon became the only medium for his ongoing poetry, short stories, and progressive philosophical treatises.

His earlier interests in handwriting analysis resulted in a two-year presidency at the Ontario Chapter of the International Graphoanalysis Society. He was also successful in his professional life, becoming a supervisor in research and development for a large mining company.

Jiri's main dedication was sealed, however, when he established Cosmic Trend Press in 1983. Cosmic Trend started with publishing Jiri's music and later numerous poetry anthologies. The early anthologies were illustrated by his daughter, Aida, and his second wife, Joyce Charrey, as well as her daughter Kaline Charrey. What made Cosmic Trend anthologies unique were the accompanying audio cassettes of Jiri's music and his narration of selected poems. Soon participating narrators emerged, most notably Joanna Nealon, a prolific poet from Massachusetts, who, being blind, memorized many poems by other poets and sent her masterful recordings to Canada. Cosmic Trend also published numerous special projects profiling selected poets over the span of two decades.

Now IN Publications is honored to present a new edition of Jiri Jirasek's comprehensive 2006 poetry collection, "Soul Estates", which covers many of his past contributions to anthologies, as well as previously unpublished poems of a more inward nature.

www.ingramcontent.com/pod-product-compliance
Lightning Source LLC
Chambersburg PA
CBHW031525040426
42445CB00009B/396